THE IRRESISTIBLE VALUE PROPOSITION

The
Irresistible
Value
Proposition

MAKE THE CUSTOMER WANT
WHAT YOU'RE SELLING

and want it NOW!

Steve Thompson

VALUE LIFECYCLE™

THE IRRESISTIBLE VALUE PROPOSITION
Make the Customer Want What You're Selling and Want It Now

ISBN   978-1-5445-0196-3 *Paperback*
       978-1-5445-0197-0 *Ebook*

Contents

FOREWORD 9

1. WHAT ARE YOU REALLY COMPETING
   AGAINST? 15

2. CAN YOU WIN THIS DEAL? 29

3. WHAT IS VALUE TO THE CUSTOMER? 55

4. CREATING AN IRRESISTIBLE VALUE
   PROPOSITION 67

5. CASE STORY CONCLUSION 73

   SUMMARY 91

   ABOUT THE AUTHOR 95

   APPENDIX 97

Foreword

"I really hate to tell you this, but we've decided to award the business to your competitor. I know you've worked hard for our business, but we've decided that ACME Corp. is simply a better fit for our business. I'm sorry, but the decision has been made."

Your primary business contact wished you luck, and when she hung up the phone, the silence was deafening. What just happened? This was your biggest opportunity for the quarter. In fact, just one month ago, your team did a terrific job on the proof of concept, and you were told by the same business contact that, technically, your solution ranked number one. To make matters worse, your boss had repeatedly reminded you that this was a "must-win" opportunity for you and your team. You have a lot of explaining to do, as sales management—not to mention your spouse—will want to know why you just lost this key deal!

At the end of the day, this disappointing outcome can be chalked up to one simple fact: the customer did not buy from you because *they didn't see the value of your offer.*

Have you ever lost a key deal you were sure you had in the bag? Does your success—in the "field" or as a manager—increasingly rely on winning a handful of critical must-win deals?

If so, this book is for you, as it is for every sales professional making a living in the B2B world—finding, positioning, proposing, negotiating, and closing critical deals with other businesses. After all, your job is only getting harder as customers have unprecedented (and growing) access to information about your products *and your other customers.* Add to that the increasing complexity of solutions being offered and the growing number of key buying influencers on the customer side, all of which introduces a huge dose of uncertainty into the equation.

Who are these influencers?

What is important to each of them?

And what if they are not fully aligned (which is almost certainly the case)?

For two decades I have developed and grown my consulting business around B2B deals, supporting more than $15 billion in over 120 different industries. I have done this for both selling *and* buying organizations. And with the increasing complexity of B2B sales, which also impacts subsequent negotiations and influences account management after the sale, I have observed that the salespeople who are likely to win more business are the ones who can manage uncertainty, reduce risk, and make it easier for the customer to make a buying decision that *they feel comfortable with.*

Now, let's revisit our deceptively simple premise: Customers choose you and award you the business because they see the value of your offer. If they don't, it's because they don't see the value. That's it. But these outwardly simple statements are *deceptive* because of the difficulty of both understanding and communicating your *value*— specifically through a value proposition. That's what this book is about: gaining a deep understanding of your value and communicating that value in an irresistible value proposition that will make your customer excited about what you're offering.

But let's be clear: The customer being excited about your offering is *not* the same as closing the deal. You must also manage uncertainty and risk before you can close, and we will address these skills later in this series of books (see the sidebar).

This book, the second in the five-part *Must-Win Deals* series, addresses an all-too-common challenge we present to the customer: an unclear—or uncompelling—value proposition. The first book, *Must-Win Deals*, reveals the four key things we, as sellers, do to make it challenging for customers to award us key deals. It also explores the idea of pursuing not just any deal, but a Great Deal. The next book, *The Compelling Proposal*, showcases the proposal as a strategic tool to reinforce trust and credibility, making it easy for the customer to buy from you (and trust their choice) and manage the uncertainty inherent in the real world. *The Painless Negotiation* then explores capturing the value in not just any deal, but a great deal for you and your customer. The final title, *Can't-Lose Accounts*, delves into delivering the promised value, which makes renewals simple, referrals enthusiastic, and upselling and cross-selling much easier. I hope you derive great value from this journey!

As I mentioned, about half of my work involves training and consulting on the buying side. As a result, my viewpoint allows me to bring you an invaluable perspective from the *other* side of the table. In these engagements I help procurement specialists, purchasing managers, and business executives at some of the largest companies in the world to position and negotiate better and more strategic deals with their key suppliers. Working with these organizations, I have developed a simple but powerful framework that represents the *customer's* view of an ideal journey—one that results in a mutually beneficial, long-term business relationship.

If my career as a salesperson, sales manager, consultant, trainer, and author has taught me one thing, it is that if a customer wants to buy in a certain way, it is generally a lot easier to sell to them that way rather than forcing them to conform to the way I would like to sell. I have also found that world-class sales organizations share a common trait: they execute—day in and day out. And the fundamentals of execution drive more success than any other factor.

But it's important to note that this is *not* a new sales process we are introducing. Instead, the *Must-Win Deals* series follows an overarching framework called the Value Lifecycle™, which looks at how the customer views an ongoing business relationship and the critical things they need from you and your organization to award you the business and retain you as a valued supplier. Our objective is to focus on those critical few outputs or customer interactions that are key to executing *any* sales process. Thus, whatever your current process may be, we are simply "supercharging" it to ensure effective execution.

A wise person once said, "Strategy without tactics is the slowest route to victory. Tactics without strategy is the noise before defeat."[1] In *The Irresistible Value Proposition*, I will provide you with the strategy (to win the business) and the right tactics (value creation and value propositions)—the critical elements that, executed well, will

---

[1]   Sometimes attributed to Sun Tzu, but possibly apocryphal, this quotation does not appear in any print translation of Sun Tzu. The first citation in Google Books is from 2002; no citation in Google Books occurs in a translation of Sun Tzu. See WikiQuotes.

make it easier for the customer to get excited about, and want, what you are selling.

But before tackling the subjects of value creation and value propositions, let's first understand the context in which value is created by determining *what we are really competing against*.

CHAPTER 1

What Are You Really Competing Against?

The Customer's Most Likely Alternative to You

When you are selling, the customer wants you to *create the potential for value*, both for them as individuals and for their business (Figure 1.1). It's really that simple. But let's not confuse *simple* with *easy*, because selling into a complex B2B environment is anything but, and it is getting more challenging by the day. What sellers too often overlook is that it is *also getting more challenging for buyers to make informed buying decisions*—and feel confident they have made the right decision for them and their business. In this environment, the seller who focuses on creating value for the customer, manages the complexity and uncertainty in the buying process, and presents a clear and compelling value proposition to the customer is at a distinct advantage.

That is where I want you to be.

THE VALUE LIFECYCLE™ IN BUSINESS RELATIONSHIPS
Managing Value Throughout the Customer Relationship

Figure 1.1

As you learned in *Must-Win Deals: How to Close Them (and why we lose them)*, while customers are *paying for* your products and services, what they are *buying* are outcomes. *Everything* revolves around the outcomes your customer wants to achieve. From a value perspective, you must translate the outcomes that are important to your customer (and you) into the right bundle of deal levers. You do this by first looking at the opportunity and saying that *a deal is going to happen*, then determining what a great deal looks like. This allows you to start forming a picture of the target you should be aiming at for both your company and your customer. In short, the goal is not to close just any deal but to try to close a *great deal.*

PAYING FOR VS. BUYING: WHY THE WORDS MATTER

This may seem like a pointless exercise in semantics, but there's a big upside to parsing the language here. Instead of dwelling on the technical or literal differences between *paying for* and *buying,* it is more important that we learn the difference between a transactional mindset, where we pay for things, and a consultative one, where we buy them. This simple distinction is easy to remember, and thus serves as a constant reminder to focus on value (better outcomes), first and foremost.

Understanding the potential value you can create for your customer begins with determining the alternative you are being compared to. That's why, as a seller, the second way that you should look at any potential opportunity is to say *no deal is going to happen,* then determine the most likely alternative each side must accept. If this sounds self-defeating—after all, we are paid to *win* deals—stay with me, for to truly understand the selling situation and the potential value you can provide, you must first understand what happens to each side if there is *no deal.*

For you, as a seller, there is only one alternative:

→ Lose the deal (and sell elsewhere).

Nine times out of ten, losing the deal is a bad thing. After all, no one built a sales career or got rich losing deals. However, lost revenue is only the "teaser headline" to the real story of what losing the deal means. The full meaning comes from a deeper examination of all the *impacts of losing* in light of the outcomes important to each side. These impacts are both business and personal, tangible and intangible. Tangible impacts are those that can be quantified or measured. Intangible impacts are very real, but we can't measure them.

For instance, the tangible impacts of losing a deal may be lost revenue for your company, no commission check, or failure to meet quota, while intangible impacts might include damage to your relationship with your customer or to your company's market image. You may also damage your relationship with your boss or even take a political hit. I can assure you that most salespeople understand, at a visceral level, the impact of this alternative—and it is bad.

However, if this is as deep as you analyze the sale, considering just your alternative as a seller, you are only looking at half the equation (and, I would argue, the least important half). What's more, if you only focus on the negative outcomes of losing the sale, then you will be selling *scared*, and will likely do some unwise things during the sale and negotiation. A sales rep who is selling scared will "give away the farm," throwing in excessive discounts and free services to win the deal.

On the other hand, if you also explore the buyer's alternative to doing a deal with you, you're likely to find this fire-sale mentality completely unnecessary. In fact, when you compare the alternatives of each side, you will usually find the situation to be the opposite of what you were likely thinking.

So, what are the customer's most likely alternatives? Theoretically, there are three:

1. Go with the competition.
2. Do nothing (status quo or alternative uses of capital).
3. Do it themselves (in some instances).

These alternatives represent three very different sales, each of which calls for a distinct strategy *and* value proposition. What's more, each of these alternatives will result in very different negotiations. While it may not be immediately apparent at the beginning of the sales cycle, you should quickly determine which of these alternatives you are up against. One of the biggest mistakes I see account teams make is using the same selling motion in all three instances.

Consider the *do it themselves* alternative. In most cases,

before your customer will be interested in hearing about your solutions, they must address numerous political and personal issues internally—not least the personal wins for those who will no longer be *doing it themselves*. As such, this alternative is best approached by first learning about those personal and political issues that will need to be addressed before the *business* issues are of interest to the customer. This is especially true if your solution may "automate" some people out of a job. The other thing to bear in mind is that you will usually sell higher in the customer organization—not to the people who may lose their jobs—when this is the alternative.

The *do nothing* alternative is usually driven by risk avoidance (the risk of change) and sometimes sheer corporate inertia. Either way, you must address these in the selling motion long before the customer will consider the merits (features, functions, and benefits) of your solution(s). This alternative may also exist because the customer simply wants to *do nothing* in the specific area you want to sell in; there are other, higher priorities they want to attend to. In all cases you are competing against an alternative use of capital, whether human or monetary. Sellers who fail to identify, analyze, and appropriately address this alternative suffer far too many losses. That's because the selling approach must be fundamentally different, at least in the early stages, from one designed to work against a traditional competitor. In other words, sellers faced with this alternative who fail to broaden their understanding of the word "competition" are very likely to lose.

To be clear, knowing which alternative you're up against doesn't tell you what that alternative actually means to the customer, nor does it tell you their desired outcomes. But it is a necessary step to building a sales strategy best suited to beat it.

EXAMPLES OF ALTERNATIVE IMPACTS
Analyzing What Each Side Must Accept If There Is No Deal

	TANGIBLE IMPACTS		INTANGIBLE IMPACTS
Seller Alternative	• Revenue (-) • Commission (-) • Quota / Goals (-) • Opportunity Costs (-) • Market Share (-) • Reference Account (-)	• President's Club (-) • Up-sell Potential Revenue (-) • Maintain Pricing Integrity (+) • Unprofitable Deal (+)	• Relationship with Customer (-) • Personal Political Hit (-) • Corporate Market Image (-) • Difficult to re-enter Account (-) • "Ripple" Effect on Other Customers (-) • Personal / Team Confidence (-) • Internal Relationships / Credibility (-)
Buyer Alternative	• Switching Costs (+/-) • Discount (+/-) • Meet Budget (+/-) • Functionality (+/-) • Integration (+/-) • Scalability (+/-) • Support Costs (+/-)	• Time to Implement (+/-) • Operational Impacts (+/-) • Regulatory Compliance (+/-) • Breadth of Solutions (+/-) • SLAs (+/-) • Key Influencer(s) MBO, Bonus, Promotion (+/-)	• Risk of change (+/-) • User Acceptance (+/-) • Politics (+/-) • Perception of Quality (+/-) • Flexibility (+/-) • Personal / Business Relationships (+/-) • Corporate Image (+/-) • Branding Message (+/-)

Table 1.1

To fully understand what the customer's alternative means, you should analyze the impacts, good and bad, of that alternative—from both business and personal perspectives, both tangible and intangible. And you should do this through the lens of what is most important to *them* and the outcomes they are trying to achieve. Table 1.1 provides a starter list of general items to consider when analyzing each side's alternative. Note that each impact for the customer's (buyer's) alternative is followed by (+/-). This means that the impact may be better or worse for that item than what you are offering. After all, the customer's alternative must be evaluated in light of what is important to them at that point in time, and you should understand both the good and bad impacts of that alternative. It is worth emphasizing that while many of the items in this list are universal, it is just a jumping-off point and should be tailored to include industry- or business-specific items, which will greatly improve its usefulness (something I've spent many hours doing for my clients).

Consider the tangible business impact of *time to implement.* A long installation or setup period could negatively impact other critical business deadlines, likely resulting in personal political hits for those charged with meeting the deadline. The *functionality* (or performance) of your product or service could affect your customer's sales or the *KPIs/MBOs of various decision makers.*

Intangible business impacts might include *risk of change,* but consider that *customer sales* or *corporate image* could also be at risk. This is a good example of how this list is only a thought starter. You will need to apply it to your particular situation to best understand the potential impacts to your customer. For instance, personal political risk and relationships will not show up on a spreadsheet analysis. If the customer has a long-term relationship with your competitor, then you should take into account potential impacts to that relationship. Is the current relationship strong, and might the customer be loath to damage that relationship? You can't measure this, but it is a part of the full picture of the alternative you are selling against.

This full picture is something I often see salespeople fail to fully consider. For example, *XYZ Company is currently buying market share by undercutting everyone else.* But have they validated that price is the only important issue to their customers? Or, *The customer must do something because the lower-level technicians are unhappy.* But what does "unhappy" mean, and why does this matter? Then there's, *The competition's offering has more features.* But are these features more than just "bells and whistles," and do they positively impact outcomes that are important to the customer? This is a much more insightful way to look at the alternative, and it often leads to a superior sales strategy and value proposition.

Remember that the most likely alternative needs to be analyzed through the lens of what the customer is really trying to achieve (outcomes) and what is important to the key decision makers (how they will measure success). For instance, we are often told that a competitor's solution is cheaper than what we are proposing. With that in mind, consider the last few key sales you've been involved in, go back to Table 1.1, and review the potential impacts to the customer. How often do you believe that cost was the only issue or *the most important issue* at stake? (Hint: having worked with many buying organizations, I can tell you that it is rarely in the top five!)

But a word of caution: I often see one side misdiagnose the other's alternative or overrate their own. For example, when your customer believes their alternative is better, faster, and cheaper than it really is, what happens to the value you put on the table? It is diminished, sometimes dramatically! One of your crucial tasks when creating value is to ensure that you and the customer have the same view of what their alternative really means to them. In other words, you must both use the same "yardstick" to measure value.

TANGIBLE AND INTANGIBLE IMPACTS
Are They Both Important?

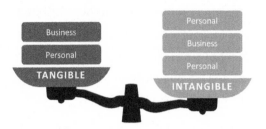

Figure 1.2

INTANGIBLE IMPACTS: IF I CAN'T MEASURE IT, DOES IT REALLY EXIST?

People often challenge me on the importance of intangible impacts. The argument typically goes like this: "All the customer really cares about are 'hard costs'—things that can be measured. They don't care about, nor do they take into account, these 'soft' items like relationships, risks, and politics." It may surprise you, but there is abundant research confirming that *most business decisions are based on intangibles*—and then decision makers try to "back into" or justify their choices by selectively using tangible impacts.

A recent study by Bain identified forty different value

dimensions in a B2B sale.[2] They then arranged these value dimensions into a hierarchy similar to Maslow's pyramid. Interestingly, the higher up in the organization the key decision makers were, the more weight they put on intangibles versus tangibles. In short, intangibles often proved more important than tangibles when it came to making most business decisions (see Figure 1.2). This is another reason we have job security in sales. Very often, the most important decision criteria can't be formulated on a spreadsheet or plotted on a graph, and our job is to discover—and sell to—these important intangibles. I can assure you, they are very real (see the sidebar).

2   Eric Almquist, Jamie Cleghorn, and Lori Sherer, "The B2B Elements of Value," *Bain*, February 20, 2018, https://www.bain.com/insights/the-b2b-elements-of-value-hbr/.

Let's say you are looking to buy a new car and you've found the exact model with all the features you want at a dealership three miles from your home. But an online search turns up another dealership a hundred miles away with the exact same car—and it's $300 cheaper. Would you drive a hundred miles to save $300? That's not a trivial amount of money, but maybe you are too busy and it's not worth your time. Or you just can't see packing up the kids for a four-hour round trip, or your current car gets awful gas mileage and kills too much of the savings. At the end of the day, you just don't see the value.

Now, what if the dealership located a hundred miles away will save you $5,000? This time the incremental value is probably too big to ignore, and I bet you'd make the trip. With that in mind, if I were to gradually drop the savings of $5,000 by $100 increments, at what point would you decide that driving a hundred miles was not worth it?

Everyone will make this decision at a different point as the savings incrementally decrease. Each individual looks at their alternative and weighs the tangible costs (time, gas, etc.) and the intangible costs (hassle, riding four hours with the kids, etc.) differently, and their point of value equilibrium will differ! Perhaps your best friend lives in the same town as the dealership, and the excuse for a road trip makes the time and cost savings on the vehicle irrelevant.

That's why you must not focus on only tangible impacts or a single issue, like price, but rather understand your customer's alternative in terms of what is important to them (business and personal) at that specific point in time. This is what you are really competing against.

By now, you may be wondering why we got onto this subject of alternatives and their analysis, but hang in there! It is one of the most important tasks in qualifying an opportunity and positioning your value during the sale and later during the negotiation. Let's see if it can help answer one of the most elusive questions in any sale: can you win?

CHAPTER 2

Can You Win This Deal?

If So, What Is the Best Strategy?

I have conducted many win-loss analyses after the completion of a sales campaign, but most of these engagements were to determine why the deal was lost. As you might imagine, when my clients win, they are too busy celebrating to analyze what happened! Why fix it if it ain't broke, right?

But I submit that it is more important to analyze *successful* deals to determine how and why you won. Instead of celebrating your short-term bookings or parsing tactics on lost deals, you should be studying the decisions and processes that enabled you to win important deals so that you can win more of them, more consistently. This is precisely what I have spent much of my career doing, and over the years I have developed a set of straightforward questions designed to help you determine *if a deal is winnable* by analyzing the alternatives to *not* doing a deal.

DOES YOUR OFFERING PROVIDE MORE VALUE THAN THE CUSTOMER'S MOST LIKELY ALTERNATIVE?

Answering this question is critical to *fully qualifying* any opportunity, and in the next chapter we will explore in much greater detail both a definition of value and three insights that help build the context for determining what value is to the customer. Put simply, you can only win a deal if, from the customer's perspective, you are able to provide *more value than their most likely alternative*.

More than once I've seen a year's time and upwards of a million dollars go into a large, complex sales campaign, only to see the deal lost. But when I ask what alternative the seller was facing, and then together we determine the impacts of that alternative, nine times out of ten the alternative was better than what my client was able to offer. Looking through the lens of what was really important to the customer's key decision makers (outcomes), it was clear my client was never going to beat that alternative.

So when should the account team have uncovered that information? Obviously, very early in the sales cycle, as there was no reason to pursue a deal they'd never win. The best sales organizations are very quick to qualify out when they realize this. They either walk (or run) away, or they try to significantly change the game—that is, change the decision criteria in their favor.

WHO REALLY NEEDS THIS DEAL?

When you evaluate both sides' alternatives to doing a deal, you should be able to answer this key question. Generally speaking, it will be whichever side has the ugliest and/or most painful alternative. Again, as the seller, your alternative is almost always bad (typically because you don't have enough qualified sales pipeline), so in most cases, you really need the deal. But what if the customer's alternative is also painful? If so, they will be motivated to do a deal with you rather than accept their alternative, and both sides should work hard to make a deal happen. Remember, you can't truly understand the dynamics of the sale—and answer the question, *who really needs this deal?*—unless you understand how painful the alternative is for *both sides.*

WHO HAS THE POWER?

When I ask sales reps who has the power in a selling situation, most say, "the customer."

Why?

"Because they have the money—and we want it." But is that really true? (See sidebar.)

This example may be a bit extreme, but it makes a key point. Let's say you've had a very successful year, and you and some colleagues are celebrating with an extreme adventure vacation deep in the jungles of Central America. You know, one of those trips where you zipline through tree canopies and over gorges, kayak whitewater rapids, explore caves and underground rivers, and excavate remote ruins.

Things go decidedly wrong when, deep in the jungle, several days travel from the nearest medical facility, you're bitten by a deadly poisonous snake. If you don't receive the anti-venom within a couple of hours, you're as good as dead. Your situation (alternative) is looking really bad! But don't give up hope just yet.

I walk into your campsite and in my backpack is the anti-venom you need. You are the "buyer" in this situation, and you have the money, so we are about to negotiate a sale. If we don't reach an agreement, what are the odds someone else will walk into your campsite with the anti-venom in the next two hours? My alternative is that I lose this sale, but I also know I'll encounter plenty more adventure-seeking people—and those snakes aren't going anywhere.

Setting aside ethics and human decency for a moment, who really has the power here? It's certainly not the buyer (you)!

Which side has the power in any sale and subsequent negotiation? Simply stated, it's the side that can walk away from a deal with the least pain—meaning the one with the better alternative. But you can only understand the attractiveness of any alternative by first evaluating the impacts of that alternative, both positive and negative. So how do you improve your power in any sale? Since power is a function of each side's alternative, there are only two moving parts here. You can *improve your alternative*, which means having a robust, qualified sales pipeline. (We'll explore this dynamic in more detail in the fourth book in the *Must-Win Deals* series.) Or you can *make the customer's alternative worse* by making your offering so valuable, they won't think about going in another direction. (That is the topic of this book and is detailed in chapter 4.)

WHAT IS YOUR VALUE PROPOSITION?

The negative impacts of your customer's alternative should provide strong clues for building an irresistible value proposition. For instance, one key pain point of the alternative may be the large resources (manpower, time, etc.) required to operate and maintain the competitor's solution. Even if the alternative is less expensive (initially) than your offering, you may want to adopt a strategy that features your automation, focusing the value proposition on saving human resources, money, and time, highlighting the downstream savings over the competition.

What if the competition is offering the latest greatest technology with dazzling features and functions, all at an attractive price point? At first glance, your situation may look dire, but further analysis shows that most of those bells and whistles are "nice-to-haves" and don't help the customer achieve their desired outcomes. Further, you determine that their complex solution will not seamlessly and easily integrate with the customer's current infrastructure, which is one of the strengths of your offering. In this case, your value proposition should highlight the reduced risk and complexity of your solution, which also achieves their critical outcomes.

The same negative impacts should also drive your strategic approach to the opportunity, but which strategy you choose will depend on the strength of your alternative, among other factors.

CHOOSING THE BEST SALES STRATEGY

Many excellent books have been written on sales strategy, so we won't spend much time on it here. However, since sales strategies are basically derived from military strategy (something I know about from direct experience), let's look at the pitfalls of not considering your strategy in the context of the alternative you are competing against. Refer to Figure 2.1.

SALES STRATEGY
How We Will Beat the Alternative

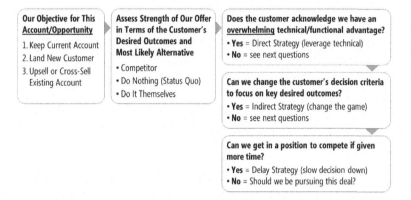

Our Objective for This Account/Opportunity	Assess Strength of Our Offer in Terms of the Customer's Desired Outcomes and Most Likely Alternative	Does the customer acknowledge we have an overwhelming technical/functional advantage?
1. Keep Current Account 2. Land New Customer 3. Upsell or Cross-Sell Existing Account	• Competitor • Do Nothing (Status Quo) • Do It Themselves	• **Yes** = Direct Strategy (leverage technical) • **No** = see next questions **Can we change the customer's decision criteria to focus on key desired outcomes?** • **Yes** = Indirect Strategy (change the game) • **No** = see next questions **Can we get in a position to compete if given more time?** • **Yes** = Delay Strategy (slow decision down) • **No** = Should we be pursuing this deal?

Figure 2.1

When you're building a sales strategy, start with your sales objective for the account or opportunity. Are you trying to retain or keep a customer? Convert or steal a customer from the competition? Further penetrate an existing customer by upselling or cross-selling additional products and services? Based on your sales objective, you must assess your relative strength and the position of your proposed offering in light of the outcomes the customer is trying to achieve today and their most likely alternative. Then you are ready to adopt one of three basic sales strategies. Let's explore each in a bit more detail.

Direct Strategy: This is the simplest strategy and the one I see most commonly used by sales reps, but too often and at the wrong times. As the name implies, a direct strategy involves an assault on the decision criteria established by the customer or the alternative. Usually boiling down to a feature, function, or price "beauty contest," this strategy can be successful, but only when you have an overwhelming technical advantage. Think of yourself as an army assaulting a well-defended fort at the top of a hill. There is no way you will succeed unless you have an overwhelming numerical advantage.

Unfortunately, in any competitive industry you will almost never have this kind of advantage for any length of time. Unless you have the latest, greatest widget or service that everyone wants, you will rarely succeed with a direct strategy. Even when you do win, odds are it will be with significant discounting. That's why customers try to force vendors into a direct strategy when they issue an RFP. They nearly always require some sort of table or form to be filled out so that they can do a side-by-side comparison.

For these reasons, I rarely recommend a direct sales strategy to my clients. But rare is not never, and this strategy can be effective when the alternative is a competitor *and* the customer recognizes that you have an overwhelming technical advantage.

Indirect Strategy: An indirect strategy involves "changing the game," or more to the point, changing the decision criteria the customer uses to make a buying decision. Your goal is to make the decision criteria about the *desired outcomes* rather than features and functions or price (or both), thus changing the game to one where you have a much higher probability of winning. For example, can you produce more or better outcomes in a set time frame? If so, you can offer a better value to the customer than features and functions or price, and you will have a significant advantage.

Again, think of an army that encounters a heavily armed fortification. Instead of directly attacking the fortification (direct strategy), which is what the defenders are counting on, your army simply goes around it. This usually causes the defenders to come out and pursue, giving your army the opportunity to choose the most advantageous time and place of battle. In a sales context, an indirect strategy is reframing the engagement to improve your chance of winning. Your first objective should be to convince the customer that the decision should be about their desired outcomes; then you are in a better position to influence the customer's view of which outcomes are most important to them (hopefully those advantageous to you).

An indirect strategy, when engaged early in the customer's buying process, is usually the best choice and typically yields superior close rates and economics (reduced discounts)—especially in a highly competitive industry. At this stage, it can be very effective against any of the three potential alternatives. For example, when dealing with a competitive alternative, your goal is to make the decision criteria about desired superior outcomes you can produce versus, perhaps, the latest features and functions the competitor is touting.

Against *do nothing* (status quo) you are battling risk of change and corporate inertia. Your objective is to first paint a picture of a desirable future state (good outcomes) that is unattainable without change. Then show the customer that you understand the risks of change and are prepared to manage and mitigate those risks together with them. Only then will they be interested in hearing about how your solution will deliver the desired outcomes.

Against *do it themselves*, start by considering the people who are currently "doing it themselves." What are the personal wins in it for them? What are the potential risks to them if the business adopts your solution? How might you maximize the personal wins and reduce the personal risks for these people? Doing this first will identify and cultivate an audience more receptive to the solutions and approaches you are proposing.

In each of these instances, you are helping the customer define the outcomes that should be important to them, and the earlier in the sales process you start the conversation, the better your chances of winning using an indirect strategy.

Delay Strategy: If you come late to the game, this may be the best strategy to adopt. It can help you gain time to better understand the alternative and position your solution and your company. But the success of this strategy depends on having enough time and using your time wisely to change the game in your favor. For instance, you might employ an indirect strategy to better position the deal. If you are unable to delay the decision process and timeline, then ask yourself if this opportunity is even worth pursuing, given the likely very low chance of winning.

You must make a conscious choice of the sales strategy you intend to employ. And guard against adopting or being forced into a strategy that does not give you the greatest chance for success. Since your customers are really buying different outcomes, you should be selling the solutions that will produce the very best outcomes— using *their* language and metrics. And it is worth repeating that the success of those outcomes is how your value will ultimately be measured.

To better illustrate the concept of *most likely alternative* and what a process of adopting the best sales strategy looks like, let's get back to our case story from the previous book.

* * *

CASE STORY CONTINUED

CAST OF CHARACTERS—RECAP

1. **Paul Stockard:** *Agile Sales Rep:* Paul is the sales rep for Agile Information Solutions (Agile), and has been calling on Worldwide Financial Solutions, Inc. (Worldwide) for the past five months. Today, Worldwide is in the process of being acquired by Mega Financial Services (MFS), creating potentially the largest opportunity Agile has ever pursued.

2. **Jane Jones:** *Agile Sales Engineer:* Jane handles all the technical aspects of an opportunity and manages proof-of-concept tests with a customer prior to a sale. She also supports the customer after the sale.

3. **Douglas Hand:** *Agile Lead Engineer for Services and Support:* Doug is responsible for implementation after the sale, as well as customer support. If Agile is chosen, he and his team will lead the integration project.

4. **Jared Carlisle:** *Agile Senior Financial Analyst:* Jared's job is to ensure that any Agile offering will be profitable to the company as well as in line with deals given to other customers. He also helps account teams quantify the value they expect to deliver to customers.

5. **Caroline Borders:** *Agile VP of Legal:* Caroline is an experienced attorney who is savvy in the technology space and handles most legal negotiations of contracts, terms, and conditions with customers.

6. **Tim Rosser:** *Agile VP of Sales:* Tim is an experienced IT sales executive who is known to be unflappable, as well as a great coach and mentor. Paul and his team have a very good relationship with Tim.

7. **Susan Renly:** *Worldwide Chief Information Officer (CIO):* Susan has been a long-time supporter of Agile and Paul. The recent acquisition of Worldwide by Mega Financial Services (MFS) has created a terrific career opportunity for her as she is in the running for the position of CIO of MFS. (The current CIO recently left the company.) This would be a significant jump in responsibility and pay, and seems contingent on the successful integration of Worldwide into MFS.

8. **Bill Sellers:** *MFS SVP of Operations:* Bill heads up the steering committee and has been charged by the MFS Board of Directors with completing the Worldwide IT integration in less than four months. It appears he has been given significant incentives to do so, as he is anxious to get this integration underway. Paul has yet to meet with Bill.

9. **Jack Grossman:** *MFS VP of Technology:* Also on the steering committee, Jack's role is to determine the integration approach. Paul, who has yet to meet Jack, has heard that he is also in the running for the newly

open MFS CIO position. Jack is a big supporter of JCN, the primary competition for the opportunity, so Paul does not expect him to be an advocate for Agile or their approach.

10. **Stephanie Holder:** *MFS Sr. Procurement Manager:* MFS has a reputation as a very tough negotiator, and Stephanie is a big reason for that. It also appears that the procurement department wields a lot of influence and power at MFS. Paul and Stephanie have not met.

* * *

Paul Stockard is a sales rep for Agile Information Solutions (Agile), a $1 billion provider of cutting-edge software and storage as a service (SaaS) solutions. Paul's key account, Worldwide Financial Solutions, Inc. (Worldwide), was recently acquired by Mega Financial Services (MFS), one of the largest financial services businesses in the world.

The acquisition has thrown into doubt what Paul thought would be a sure renewal, and he reached out to **Susan Renly**, Worldwide's CIO and a strong Agile supporter, for guidance. Susan reassured Paul that Agile was still a lock for the renewal. In fact, the papers had already been drawn up. But with MFS now in the picture, a much larger opportunity had presented itself, one that played directly to Agile's strength as a SaaS-based solution provider. MFS needed to on-board Worldwide's technology—quickly—and it was assumed that they would go their usual route, using JCN, their entrenched technology solution provider, to port everything to their on-premises infrastructure "behind the firewall."

But Susan saw an opportunity to leverage Agile's position as Worldwide's preferred technology provider—one with a more nimble and forward-looking solution set—while also advancing her professional prospects. If she could pull off a win for Agile, she had a very good shot at landing the recently vacated CIO position at MFS.

There was just one catch, and it was a big one. With MFS's acquisition of Worldwide, Agile now had a built-in competitor in JCN. As the incumbent technology supplier for MFS, JCN was not going to go down without a fight, and Agile represented a direct threat to their dominant position as MFS's preferred provider.

Paul and his sales team did a deep dive on both MFS and JCN, and working with Susan, they determined that the key decision-makers would be in the C-suite, given that this was chiefly an issue of customer retention and revenue growth versus a more straightforward IT "technology" opportunity.

Susan's position on the Worldwide steering committee

gave her, and by extension Paul, access to a key mentor within the organization, **Bill Sellers**. Paul's team pulled off an important and successful proof-of-concept demonstration, after which Susan, fresh from a steering committee meeting, brought Paul some hugely important news from the meeting: the integration had to be flawless, and it had to be done quickly—so quickly, in fact, that there was some question as to whether JCN would be able to pull it off in the prescribed time frame dictated by the Board of Directors. Suddenly, Agile appeared to be in a much stronger position to contemplate a successful campaign against a strong incumbent, and Paul and the team now had to scramble to put together a strategy in a few short days.

Thankfully, Paul's initial negotiation with the internal group at Agile went smoothly. The group consisted of **Tim Rosser**, VP of sales; **Jared Carlisle**, senior financial analyst; **Doug Hand**, lead engineer for services and support; and **Caroline Borders**, Agile's VP of legal. The group agreed on what a great deal would look like for both Agile and MFS (based on the information they had to date), enabling Paul to go back to his team with a prioritized list of deal levers and limits that would enable them to position the right deal for Agile and MFS.

All things considered, they were as prepared as they could possibly be at this stage, but there was much more they needed to validate, not least the outcomes important to MFS, in particular to Bill Sellers. They also needed to be sure that JCN was the real alternative they were competing against and sort out what that meant to MFS (impacts).

Susan Renly called Paul for their daily check-in on the status of the MFS acquisition.

"Paul, listen," she began urgently. "I've heard from **Jack Grossman** that JCN is offering to do the Worldwide integration by *giving away* their competing software and services...absolutely free! As you can imagine, Jack seemed pretty happy to pass along this little bombshell," she added, sarcastically.

"Good to know...I think?" Paul quipped. He wondered silently how—or whether—Agile could compete with "free." At least now he had confirmation that MFS's alternative was JCN, and at this point that alternative did not look promising for Agile. And as Susan had previously mentioned, JCN had demonstrated a capacity for doing almost anything to keep SaaS firms out of their accounts as they profited not only from hardware and software but also services. Paul expected a tough fight, and the "race to zero" bait was just a shot across the bow.

"I know, right?" Susan echoed. "This is a major hurdle,

and I can't help but think it might make the decision to select JCN an easy one, at least for the rest of the committee. Not to mention what it would mean for Jack's goal of being named CIO at MFS!"

"Right," Paul said slowly, his thoughts shifting midword from reactive to strategic. JCN's offer to MFS meant that he and the account team needed to take a big step back and analyze the alternative that Agile was competing against.

"This definitely feels like a setback," he continued, "but I'm not throwing in the towel. I need to get together with my team and take a clear-eyed look at everything that we now know. After all, free is never really free, is it? With that in mind, we'll be meeting later today, and we'll need to settle on our approach and strategy."

He told Susan that he would reconnect with her as soon as he had more information. To be sure, Paul couldn't afford to fall into the trap of competing head-to-head with JCN on *their* terms. If JCN was giving the software and services away, then Agile would have to *pay* MFS to take their solution—obviously not a proposition that Paul's sales management would embrace. But now, with the information they had on the outcomes important to MFS and Bill Sellers, it was time to dig in to the alternative analysis for this opportunity.

An hour later, Paul gathered his team in the conference room for a session to analyze both Agile's alternative to doing a deal with MFS and MFS's alternative to doing a deal with Agile. MFS's clear alternative was JCN, but what did that really mean?

Paul's account team included **Jane Jones**, Doug Hand, and Jared Carlisle, the senior financial analyst. He wasted no time filling them in on the progress to date and what he knew from his latest conversations with Susan Renly.

"In short," Paul began, "we believe we know what MFS is trying to solve for. We also believe we know what's important to Bill Sellers, the key decision maker. And it looks pretty certain that we are competing with JCN. Now we need to determine if this is a qualified opportunity for Agile, and if so, how we're going to win it."

Paul then reminded the team, "We have to start by assuming that MFS will not do a deal with Agile, and our job is to determine the most likely alternative for each side and what those alternatives mean to each side. To do that, we have to analyze the impacts that we can measure—the tangible ones—as well as the ones we can't. But remember that the intangible impacts are still very real, and the fact that we can't measure them could play to our advantage!"

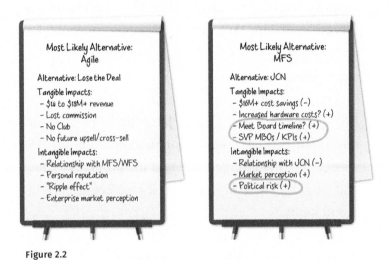

Figure 2.2

Jane, Doug, Jared, and Paul busied themselves for the better part of an hour and finally arrived at a couple of flip charts (Figure 2.2) showing the tangible and intangible impacts of each party's alternative.

"As we know," Paul continued, gesturing to the Agile chart, "our only alternative to doing a deal is to lose the deal. But looking at the impacts of losing the deal—that's when things really start to get ugly!"

He went to the flip chart and detailed the *tangible* impacts of losing the deal:

→ Lose the largest opportunity in the company's history, representing from $14 million to $18 million in potential total revenue.

→ Lose the largest commission checks of our careers.

→ No Club this year

→ Agile misses out on significant future growth opportunities if MFS acquires more companies.

The team then analyzed the *intangible* impacts to losing the deal with MFS. While not quantifiable, the intangibles were very real and just as painful:

→ Likely damage both to the team's relationship with Susan Renly and to Paul's chances of establishing a relationship with MFS

→ A critical hit to the professional reputations of Paul and the team members within Agile for losing the company's largest opportunity to date. Management could very well bust Paul down to small account sales, irreparably damaging his career.

→ The ripple effect of the loss through industry news and blogs, which could impact other deals in the current SMB market

→ Significant and potentially lasting negative repercussions in the enterprise market, where Agile is looking to grow the business

As they reviewed and absorbed what losing this deal with MFS could mean for both the company and for their careers, the mood darkened a bit. But Paul injected a little perspective.

"Look, this is why we get the big bucks," he said. "And let's not forget, our alternative is almost always ugly. Let's just stay focused and keep our fingers crossed that an analysis of the MFS alternative turns up something useful!"

Everyone agreed that for MFS, *doing nothing* or *doing it themselves* were not viable alternatives in this case. Their only option was a competitor, and JCN was clearly the leading candidate. Susan had already backgrounded Paul, so he briefed the team.

"JCN works with virtually every large enterprise around the globe. They provide critical hardware, software, consulting, and support services. The company's *modus operandi* is to establish strong executive relationships with their clients, and MFS is no exception. This is easily the most formidable competitor we have ever faced!"

The team then carefully considered the *tangible* impacts of MFS choosing JCN:

→ "Free software and services" yielding approximately $16 million in cost savings to MFS—a big minus for Agile
→ JCN software that must be installed on JCN hardware

to work, incurring an estimated hardware expenditure of between $30 million and $40 million—potentially a big plus for Agile

→ Estimated time to obtain and configure the hardware, including migration of Worldwide databases and applications, of six to ten months—maybe a very big plus for Agile!

→ Bill Sellers' incentives to meet the board's deadline—a big plus given JCN's installation timeline

Of course, $16 million in savings out of the box would be a strong opener for JCN, but the savings would be more than offset by the cost of their proprietary hardware. And if the money math were not bad enough, their installation timeline—at least two months beyond the board's deadline—would bring JCN's viability into much more critical light, which was good news for Paul and his team.

What's more, the board had made the importance of meeting the deadline very clear to Bill Sellers, and Paul suspected that Bill had been given incentives, most likely stock options, a bonus, or a promotion, if he could bring the project in on time. This could be very important to Agile's value proposition and sales strategy.

The team's analysis of the *intangible* impacts yielded similar results in that some things worked for Agile and others against them:

→ MFS's desire to maintain a good relationship with JCN—a negative for Agile

→ Potential for negative market perceptions of MFS if JCN is unable to meet the integration deadline—potentially a big plus for Agile

→ Significant political risk to Bill Sellers and the steering committee if they fail to finish the integration on time—maybe the biggest plus for Agile

MFS and JCN shared both a long history doing business together and many powerful high-level connections, in addition to Jack Grossman. As a result, even with the tangible costs and risks of choosing JCN for this project, MFS would think long and hard before putting that relationship at risk. But they would also have to consider the cost, both in stock value and reputation, of missing market expectations in the event of a delayed integration, with implications that would go all the way to the CEO. For his part, Bill Sellers faced considerable career peril if he missed the board's objectives, and Paul was betting that he would not risk choosing a vendor that would almost certainly go over the all-important deadline.

As painful as it was to discuss the possibility of losing this deal, the analysis was productive, and Paul now believed the team had much better insight into the right sales strategy and perhaps a potential winning value proposition.

Looking at each side's alternative, the team deduced that MFS would likely have a slight edge in power in any negotiation. Though Agile's alternative appeared to be a bit worse, the alternative for each side was still plenty painful, so some kind of deal was compelling for both parties. Clearly, the most important pain point of the MFS alternative was the board's timeline. While some vetting was still in order, it all came down to the time needed for Agile's account team to implement their cloud-based solution versus JCN's on-premises hardware and software solution.

As with any review session, the most important outputs were the action items, so Paul tasked his team with getting the answer to two questions as quickly as possible:

→ How long would it take JCN to implement their solution?
→ How quickly could the account team implement Agile's solution?

"We need our best thinking here," Paul said to the team, "so let's take advantage of any and all resources here at Agile. If we can answer these two questions, we'll have a much better idea of our chances against JCN—and how we might win!"

"And just one more thing," he added with mock gravity. "If we pull this off, I'm buying the drinks!"

* * *

I have not kept a tally (perhaps my editor has) of how many times I have used the word "value," but we have yet to fully define this all-important concept. Value is the overarching reason the customer will choose to buy from you. And, importantly, the more value the customer sees, the sooner they will feel compelled to close a deal. What's more, the ultimate size of the deal will likely be directly tied to the amount of value you bring.

As Mark Twain supposedly quipped, "Everyone talks about the weather, but nobody does anything about it."[3] Our goal in *The Irresistible Value Proposition* is not simply to talk about the concept of value, but to understand what it means—because *we need to do something about it!*

---

3   While there is much truth in the statement, it may surprise you that Twain did not say it. The witticism actually came from his friend Charles Dudley Warner.

CHAPTER 3

What Is Value to the Customer?

Why the Customer Will Choose You

Let's say that for the past four months you've been actively pursuing a promising new customer, one of the largest opportunities in your sales pipeline. One day, while visiting your day-to-day contact at this client, you are introduced to one of the key decision makers. Everything seems low key and cordial until he looks at you and says, "I realize you have been working with my team for a while, and they seem to like your solution. But I have to be honest with you; *I'm not sure* exactly what we're going to get out of this."

This decision maker is really asking: what is your value proposition? What's in it for me, personally and professionally and for the business?

How you respond to these questions can be the difference between winning the business and losing it, so it's no surprise that for many sales reps this moment causes deep discomfort, bordering on sheer terror. While in front of decision makers, perhaps for the first time, you may not really understand the value you are offering your customer. Or you may not be sure if your take on value is relevant to that decision maker. Or maybe you think you know your value, but on reflection, it feels more like your company's marketing material—not specific to this customer, their business needs, or what they are trying to accomplish. If you don't have the right answer to the all-important question—*what's in it for me and my business?*—then at best you have sorted yourself into the middle of the pack as a "typical vendor." Now, odds are your competitors are no better at articulating their value than you, but that just makes them your "good enough" competitors in a price-only shootout—not the place you want to be!

Instead of fearing this situation, successful salespeople embrace the challenge it represents as well as the opportunity for closing a deal quickly. In other words, they begin their selling motion with the expectation that they will have to answer this question to win the business. And they know that answering the question well will increase the odds of landing bigger deals that close faster.

THE VALUE LIFECYCLE™ IN BUSINESS RELATIONSHIPS
Managing Value Throughout the Customer Relationship

Figure 3.1

Have a look at Figure 3.1, and let's continue our discovery of value at the beginning of the Value Lifecycle™, where we create value in the mind of the customer—a process also known as "selling." Our goal is to define this thing called value and then turn it into a targeted, highly relevant value proposition. As we begin, here is some food for thought:

→ What motivates a customer to choose you and your company and to want to close a deal quickly? Simply put, it is the incremental *value they perceive!* The buyer chooses you over a competitor or another alternative because they see more value in doing business with you.

→ Furthermore, the *more value* the customer sees in doing business with you, the *more quickly* they will be motivated to close the business so that they can realize that value as soon as possible.

→ Defining value can be challenging because your typical definition as a seller is irrelevant. After all, you are not the one signing the check. *It is the customer's definition that counts*, and that is what we must discover as early as possible in the selling process.

THREE VALUE INSIGHTS

I have derived three critical insights concerning value. To explore them, let's start with a simple definition. *Merriam-Webster* (on the web) defines value as "relative worth, utility, or importance." Using this as a starting point to define value in B2B selling, your initial question might be, *relative to what?* The answer lies in our first two insights:

→ Value is, anywhere and everywhere, specific to the customer's situation and is an **impact based on the customer's desired outcomes.**

→ Value only exists in the customer's mind as the perceived utility or worth that is **incremental to the customer's next best alternative** to you.

Therefore, the products or services you sell have zero intrinsic value until the customer considers them in the context of their current situation and the outcomes they want to achieve, then decides how they compare to the next best alternative. And then it is *only the increment* that is valuable! Think about that. This statement will probably anger every marketing-message-writing, brochure-developing, social-selling, and elevator-pitch-crafting marketing professional in the business. But that's not my intent.

It's not that messaging, brochures, social campaigns, and tactical pitches aren't useful. These tools are indispensable for generating awareness and interest, as well as creating leads and potential opportunities—all traditional roles of marketing. But what they can't give you is a winning value proposition for *this customer*—based on their particular wants and needs, their situation, and relative to their alternative (more on that soon). This is a critical concept to grasp, so let's bring it to life.

Say you are stranded on a small desert island, with no food or water. You've been there for a few days, and you're in pretty bad shape. As you stand on the beach contemplating your situation, I come hovering over you in a helicopter. In one hand I have a bag with $2 million worth of diamonds, which I drop at your feet. Now, what is the value of those diamonds to you? You can't eat them, drink them, or spend them. (And no, I'm not giving you a ride.) With my helicopter I could go virtually anywhere in the world and get the equivalent of $2 million for those diamonds, but their value to you when stuck on this desert island is zero.[4]

In the other hand I have a sack with $200 worth of groceries, including bottled water and fruit juices. What is this option worth to you? Certainly more than the diamonds. In fact, it is priceless! But from my perspective, when I initially flew over the island, they were only worth about $200 in my mind. Think about that.

If this example is a little extreme, it's to make a critical point: you can't know the potential value you are providing a customer until you understand what is important to them at that moment and in that particular situation, and then you must consider the alternative against which incremental value is being created. (For a somewhat less extreme illustration, see the sidebar.)

---

4   Some of my clients point out that at least they will die rich!

You are expecting a houseful of guests in two days, and your old reliable dishwasher finally gives out. You quickly call a repairman, who arrives only to tell you that the cost of fixing the machine may be significantly more than replacing it with a new one. The parts he needs, if he can even get them, will take at least a week to arrive. Wasting no time, you visit the nearest appliance dealer and settle on a model that has all the features you want and will match your kitchen décor. The dealer is asking $650, which includes warranty, delivery, installation, and haul-away of your old dishwasher. Unfortunately, he doesn't currently have one in stock, and it will be at least five days before he can get one and install it.

So you call another appliance dealer who advertises the same brands. He informs you that he has the exact model you want in stock with the same service and warranty as the other vendor—and he can deliver the dishwasher tomorrow. The only other difference is that his price is $100 higher, which you are all too happy to pay! What is the value to you of this vendor's solution? It isn't the dishwasher itself, for the machines offered by each vendor are identical. It isn't the price, because you've enthusiastically chosen to pay $100 more. The value to you lies in the incremental difference between delivery tomorrow and delivery five days from now. With your guests showing up in two days, delivery tomorrow is worth a lot more than the additional $100. The "value" in this example is measured in time-to-installation and labor savings—yours: that is, hand-washing piles of dirty dishes (the alternative to having no dishwasher).

If you are in sales, I'm sure you've been in a situation where you are describing your product or service to a potential customer, only to have them tell you that your competition has the same basic features and offering. It's disheartening, but what they are telling you is key: you are not offering any value to them.

By contrast, when your conversation is about value (rather than features and functions), you almost never hear this response. In my practice I see too many organizations spend way too much time training salespeople to discuss features, functions, and benefits, then arming them with the famous "elevator pitch." But customers don't buy features and functions. They might *pay for* benefits, but only if those benefits *produce outcomes* that are relevant and incremental to their next best alternative. And customers only see and care about the value of these benefits if they are applicable to their current situation and are articulated in *their language*.

This leads us to our third critical insight concerning value.

→ Customers measure value in both **business and personal** terms, and for each it can be **tangible and intangible**.

Value, both tangible and intangible, can be measured in business terms. Remember, you can readily quantify and measure tangible value. But intangible value, while real, is difficult if not impossible to measure. (Perhaps more than anything, intangible value is *impractical* to quantify). For example, tangible business value could be cost reduction. But what specific costs, reduced how much, and by when? Now you are getting to the customer's specific situation and beginning to define the value on their terms. If a customer wants to improve a process, like a new product or service launch, how will they know it has improved? Perhaps it is a reduction in time to launch the product or service (time to market). What is it today, what do they want the timeline to be reduced to, and by when? Now you are starting to get to the heart of tangible value—for *this* customer.

Intangible business value could be an improvement of corporate image, or risk reduction. But how will you and the customer know that corporate image has been improved? What is the perception of risk today, and what needs to be done to improve the current risk profile? While the ability to measure intangible value may be up for debate, its importance to the business is unambiguous. In this case, you must work with the customer to define the steps or specific changes made that should result in an improved image and reduced risk.

Personal value is also seen as both tangible and intangible. For example, a particular initiative may have a bonus or promotion attached to successful completion—a very tangible personal impact. But you should understand what "successful" means to this customer because that is ultimately what will lead to the bonus or promotion, and it is how value will be measured.

An intangible personal impact may be significant political

risk or the potential to damage key relationships (with, say, senior management) if an initiative is not successful and the outcomes are not realized. Conversely, success may result in positive personal and team recognition. Note that, as with business intangibles, you cannot measure or directly produce the intangible impact. Rather, you must help the customer achieve the tangible outcomes, and the intangibles will typically follow. But as before, if you don't know what "successful" looks like to this customer, your odds of achieving the tangibles drop, causing the odds of delivering on the intangibles to drop even further. These intangible outcomes can't be quantified or captured in a spreadsheet or an ROI calculation. But make no mistake— they are very important to the customer. In short, nearly all personal value is a direct result of first achieving the desired business outcomes.

EXAMPLES OF VALUE IN THE CUSTOMER'S EYES

Business Outcomes
- Increase revenues
- Lower costs
- Process improvement
- Increase customer satisfaction
- Reduce risk, corporate image

Personal Outcomes
- Meet goals and objectives (MBOs / KPIs)
- Commission, bonus, pay raise, promotions
- Receive personal and team recognition
- Improve relationships
- Reduce political risk

Value is delivering the outcomes the customer cares about...
But doing more, better, faster, easier, cheaper, with less risk, etc. than the customer's most likely alternative (*Incremental*)

Figure 3.2

Figure 3.2 provides some examples of how a customer might measure value. Note that there are no products or services on these lists. This is because customers don't *buy* products or services. They *pay for* products and services. You may recall (from the previous book) that customers *buy* what the list items are designed to measure: outcomes. But they will only see value if the outcome you produce is incrementally better than their alternative to you—which is what you are ultimately competing against. And—this is worth repeating—they will only readily recognize your value if it is in their language (success metrics).

Now, let's go back momentarily and reflect on the analysis of the most likely alternative described in chapter 1. By conducting this analysis of the totality of *various impacts* of not doing a deal with you, you were actually determining *the value of that alternative to the customer*. Then, by comparing your offering to that alternative, you can determine the incremental value you were providing the customer.

Now that you know what *value* is in the B2B sales context, it's time to put it into a readily recognizable form the customer will relate to—an irresistible value proposition.

CHAPTER 4

Creating an Irresistible Value Proposition

Compel the Customer to Want Your Offering—Right Now!

The customer's perception of your value will enable three critical outcomes for you: you can win the business without competing on price alone, it will motivate the customer to want a big deal versus a small one, and it will motivate them to close the deal quickly.

The definitive driver of that value perception is an irresistible value proposition. To understand why a value proposition is so important, let's revisit the beginning of the previous chapter, where you are standing in front of one of the key decision makers for a potential customer with a sizable opportunity. When he says, "I'm not sure exactly what we're going to get out of this," what he is really doing is asking for your value proposition.

An irresistible value proposition makes it easier for the customer to choose you. It is essential to *both* increasing your conversion rates and compressing your sales cycle.

ATTRIBUTES OF AN IRRESITIBLE VALUE PROPOSITION

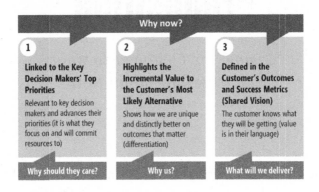

Figure 4.1

So how do you make a value proposition irresistible? As illustrated in Figure 4.1, you must first answer the question, *why should they care?* by linking it to one or more of the priorities of the key decision maker(s). This makes it highly relevant to them and lets them know why they should be listening to you. It is important to "connect the dots" to their priorities because that is what they spend money on, and there is a finite amount of money or budget in any business. I have reviewed what are presented to me as good value propositions from my clients, only to find that they focus on the customer's "priority number 99." They are compelling on paper, but irrelevant to *that* customer. Most organizations have limited resources, enough to focus on just a handful of priorities, and you are much more likely to get their attention if you target the things most important to the key decision makers. Otherwise you are trying to sell a nice-to-have.

The second attribute of a compelling value proposition answers the question, *why us?* by highlighting the *incremental value* between you and the customer's most likely alternative, cutting through the clutter and showing how you are unique and distinctly better. (You may recognize this as "differentiation," a go-to term for many sales processes). The alternative could be a competitor, but it's important to remember that the *do nothing* and *do it themselves* alternatives are always available to the customer—and each will most likely require a different form of value proposition.

If you've ever explained your product's features and functions to a buyer only to be told that your competition is offering the same things, *then you are not talking about value*. In fact, those features and functions are likely just table stakes, or the price to play in your industry, and they don't represent value to the customer. Remember, customers don't buy features or functions; they buy different outcomes or results. Your job is to highlight what is *unique* about the outcome(s) you can produce. Only your incremental value can tell the customer why they should care about you, your solutions, and your company.

The third attribute of a compelling value proposition uses the customer's success metrics to clearly answer the question, *what will we deliver?* In other words, you present value to them in their language: the outcomes they are trying to achieve, the way they talk about value, and the way they think about value. Why confuse the customer and make it hard for them to understand the value you intend to provide by speaking in a foreign language—your corporate lingo?

Taken together, these three attributes answer the question, *why now?* After all, if you focus on priority outcomes of the key decision makers, show them the incremental outcomes you are prepared to produce, and detail those outcomes in their language (success metrics), why would they not want to close the deal now? Let's look at an example of an irresistible value proposition developed by one of my clients (see sidebar).

The time frame is during the financial crisis of 2008–2009. The customer was a large international overnight shipping firm. Over a few months' time, shipping volumes had dramatically dropped to levels not seen since the 2001 recession. As a result, the shipping firm had canceled all new projects and initiatives and reduced all departmental budgets by 30 percent. For the IT department, this meant the postponement of a new data center, one desperately needed to handle the copious data generated by the business. Even worse, the current IT infrastructure was almost tapped out. They were projected to completely run out of data storage capacity within a few months. (Even with reduced shipping volumes, the business was still producing large amounts of data from tracking packages, collecting signatures, etc.)

My client provided software that efficiently managed data storage and retrieval and, most relevant to this customer, removed duplicate data, thereby reducing the amount of storage required. Our solution was the only one that worked in the customer's heterogeneous hardware environment. After analyzing the shipping firm's IT infrastructure and data profile, my client offered the following irresistible value proposition: "Your top priority is to continue to support business operations. Using our software solution, we will reduce your current data storage volume by approximately 27 percent by removing all duplicate files in your data. This will extend the life of your current IT infrastructure by at least twenty to twenty-four months." It was no more complicated than that. Let's see how this value proposition stacks up against our criteria (Figure 4.2).

Supporting the business was the number-one priority of the CIO; in fact, it was literally keeping him up at night! And the incremental value we presented (extending the life of his IT infrastructure by reducing the current volume of data by 27 percent) was an option no one else was offering. We communicated our value in the customer's language, stating that our solution could extend the useful life of their IT infrastructure for up to twenty to twenty-four months. *Why now?* was answered by the combination of all the above. This proved to be an irresistible value proposition, resulting in a seven-figure, sole-source deal that closed in a matter of a few weeks.

When I share this story with new clients, I'm often asked where the money came from. After all, every new project had been canceled and budgets had been reduced by 30 percent. Very simply, the CIO looked at current projects and initiatives that were underway and canceled several of them to free up funding for this new initiative. He canceled them because they were not providing as much value to him as our solution.

As you can imagine, my client's account team had no difficulty getting access to the CIO, someone they had never met with before. Nor was price an issue in the subsequent negotiation, which was mostly about timing and how quickly the implementation team could begin work. Our value proposition had become irresistible to the CIO.

As a postscript, we delivered the promised value and were later awarded a much larger, eight-figure, sole-source deal to solve other problems.

IRRESISTIBLE VALUE PROPOSITION
Does It Pass Our Test?

We will reduce your current data storage volume by approximately 27% by removing all duplicate files in your data. This will extend the life of your current IT infrastructure by at least 20 to 24 months.

- **Top Priority**: Extend the life of the current IT infrastructure
- **Incremental**: Software-based solution that works in heterogenous hardware environment
- **Success Metrics**: Supports the business through strategically challenging period
- **Why Now**: Our solution *buys you time* by *leveraging existing technology.*

Figure 4.2

Companies and salespeople who master the art of making it easy to buy from them are those who frame their value proposition in the customer's success metrics. They make it easy for their customers to understand what they intend to deliver. Later in the Value Lifecycle™, this will become critical to delivering the promised value and getting credit for the past value delivered (the focus of the fifth book in the *Must-Win Deals* series).

Let's turn our attention back to the case story to see how Paul and the account team will develop their irresistible value proposition and implement the right sales strategy.

CHAPTER 5

Case Story Conclusion

It appeared that JCN's real Achilles' heel was their implementation schedule, which meant that Paul and the team needed an indirect sales strategy, one that would change MFS's decision to one about time to completion instead of playing JCN's game of lowest price. Whether they had a truly qualified opportunity to pursue now came down to the two questions the team would answer that evening.

The next morning, Paul got some good news from the team. After analyzing the IT infrastructure, as well as the databases and applications at MFS, they had come up with a bold approach that would enable Agile to implement their solution in approximately five weeks! Further research showed that JCN's best-case implementation timeline would be at least five to six months—maybe as many as eight. This validated what yesterday's alternative analysis meeting seemed to be telling them, and Paul was encouraged that the team's research had borne out their conclusions. If the steering committee chose to go with JCN, they would almost certainly not meet the board's schedule, and they would have to accept the consequences of choosing that alternative.

Paul now felt that the team had the makings of a compelling value proposition and a good chance of winning the deal. But he still needed to validate everything with Bill Sellers to ensure that the timeline was indeed critical to MFS, while also making sure that the account team was as prepared as possible to deploy this indirect sales strategy.

Paul and the team had to land a direct hit with their value proposition and state exactly why MFS should choose Agile's solution. He reminded everyone that their value proposition should first demonstrate the importance of their solution to MFS by linking it to the top priorities of the key decision makers (in this case Bill Sellers and, by extension, the MFS executive team). It should also highlight the incremental value Agile added over JCN. Finally, to be irresistible, their value proposition needed to articulate what Agile would deliver, clearly and *in the customer's language* (their success metrics), to make it easy to understand. This was critical because after a successful implementation, Agile would be asking for credit for the value they delivered, and that credit would be key to landing follow-on upsell and cross-sell opportunities at MFS.

Therefore, Paul recommended that the value proposition be based on time to implement. This would address what they believed to be the steering committee's top priority. Agile's incremental value was therefore determined to be an implementation schedule of approximately one-sixth the time that JCN would need for their solution, and the team chose to highlight that this was at least two months ahead of the timeline dictated by the board.

There was much discussion about this approach, as Jared Carlisle, the senior financial analyst, insisted that the value must be "dollarized" to show the monetary value of this time savings to MFS. He concluded that completing the implementation two months ahead of schedule was likely worth a lot of money to MFS, but the team countered that there was simply no way to calculate how much with any degree of certainty. Besides, MFS had a team of analysts that could calculate this for the steering committee, so Agile's account team chose to keep it simple and to state their company's value in the success metrics Bill Sellers had already shared with Susan Renly. They agreed to revisit this issue if Paul learned anything different when he met with Bill. It was time to get Susan Renly back on the phone to set up that meeting.

At Susan's request, the Agile account team had just completed a successful proof of concept of their solution on a small part of the Worldwide and MFS infrastructure. The demonstration was completed for the IT technical team at MFS under the direction of Susan and her team at Worldwide. She was very pleased with the results and kept her promise of introducing Paul to the SVP of operations at MFS.

Susan was excited when she answered the phone: "Paul, I was just about to call you. Bill has heard about the work you and the team have been doing, and he is anxious to meet with you. In fact, this is a top priority for him, and he'd like to meet tomorrow!"

"I'm there," Paul responded without hesitation. He was pleased by the good news but hardly surprised that his experienced team had piqued Bill's interest.

"Great! I'll put you in touch with his admin," Susan replied. *This might be one of the pivotal meetings of my sales career*, Paul thought after confirming the meeting with Bill's admin.

* * *

"Bill Sellers, please meet Paul Stockard with Agile Information Solutions," Susan said, smiling as the two men shook hands warmly.

The meeting, in Bill's office at MFS, was businesslike and cordial. They chatted for a few minutes, and eventually Bill looked at Paul and said, "I know you've been working with Susan and her team for a while, and they seem to like the solution you're proposing for us. But I have to be honest, there's a lot on the line here, and I need some convincing."

Bill was asking, in no uncertain terms, *what is Agile's value proposition?* At that moment, Paul could win the business—or lose it! But Paul's account team had done their homework, and his answer was short and to the point.

"We believe Agile's solution can give your sales and account management teams complete access to Worldwide data and applications well before the board's deadline. We also believe we can help keep you under budget by eliminating or deferring approximately $30 million to $40 million in hardware costs. Of course, this timeline is based on beginning work as soon as possible."

Paul floated the middle part of his statement to determine if cost savings was truly an issue. The last part was fishing for a sense of urgency when it came to time. If his team was right, he could begin to nail down the buying steps required before a deal could be closed.

* * *

Lets' take a quick break from the case story and see how well Agile's value proposition stacks up against our criteria for being irresistible.

→ **Top Priority:** Complete access to Worldwide data and applications
→ **Incremental:** Well before the board's deadline
→ **Success Metrics:** At this point, Paul has not given any specifics in terms of how far ahead of the deadline.
→ **Why Now?:** If this initiative is as urgent as Paul and his team believe, then the answer to the question, *why now?* is self-evident since the work can't begin until the contract is awarded.

At this point, Paul can't be sure that his value proposition is irresistible, because much remains to be validated with Bill Sellers. He has hedged his bet by throwing in the potential savings of "$30 million to $40 million in hardware costs," but he must ascertain if this is meaningful or simply "icing on the cake." He also needs to understand if JCN's strategy of focusing on costs is effectively aiming at the critical target for Bill and MFS.

Let's turn back to the case story and see how Paul's value proposition fares.

* * *

Bill quickly turned to Susan, "Is this really possible?"

"Yes!" she replied confidently. "We just completed a proof of concept that demonstrated that the technology will work at MFS. And not only were the results positive, but I'm frankly surprised at how quick and trouble-free the test was." She explained that she had seen the draft Agile customer success plan and believed that the timelines were both realistic and achievable.

Turning back to Paul, Bill asked excitedly, "Are you sure this can be done ahead of the deadline?"

Don't get out too far over your skis, Paul thought.

"We are confident the deadline can be beaten by weeks— *maybe more*," he responded, cautiously stressing the last two words. "But it all depends on when the actual work begins."

"So when would Agile be ready to begin work?" Bill asked.

"Right away," Paul responded quickly. "But since this is the first time Agile has done business with MFS, the start time will depend on the remaining buying steps that MFS requires before we sign a contract."

Bill frowned. He said he was unaware that Agile did not

have a supplier contract with MFS and that getting one in place with a new supplier was always an arduous process. The legal department was involved in approving contracts, of course, but MFS's purchasing department was very powerful in the organization and had a reputation for putting suppliers through the ringer. What's more, there were certain steps, like final price negotiations with purchasing, that he simply couldn't skip, as they were part of corporate policy.

Paul was starting to feel that knot in his stomach again as the conversation took a decidedly negative turn.

"I need time to think about this," Bill concluded. "Right now I've got a meeting with the CEO. Can we reconvene in two hours to discuss potential next steps?"

Paul and Susan readily agreed to meet Bill after lunch, but now Paul was feeling there would definitely be some challenges ahead, although it still looked like Agile had a shot at winning the deal.

I wonder what else Bill needs time to think about, he thought.

Over lunch, Paul and Susan refined their objectives for the afternoon meeting, but when they arrived at the SVP's office at the appointed time, Bill was clearly agitated. He shared that the meeting with his CEO had been tense, and if anything, he was under more pressure to show progress on the Worldwide integration. It seemed the rest of the organization was moving rapidly toward the target integration date. The SVP of sales was ahead of schedule in training his team on the new Worldwide offerings, and he expected to have the entire sales and account management team trained within three months. The chief marketing officer had just briefed the CEO that the new marketing and media campaigns for the Worldwide offerings were approved and would launch in two months.

"In light of all this, the CEO was less than pleased with my progress on the integration," Bill concluded candidly. "But here's the real icing on the cake. A senior executive from JCN met with our CEO yesterday to discuss how JCN can help with the Worldwide integration. The JCN executive suggested—in the interest of time, of course—that his team present their proposal to the steering committee *this Friday*, and the CEO agreed."

Paul half blurted, "That's just three days from now!" He was clearly outflanked here politically, and his stomach was now doing somersaults.

"That's right, and I apologize for the crunch deadline," Bill responded. "I didn't have much choice. But while I agreed to the presentation by JCN, I also insisted that the steering committee entertain a proposal presentation from Agile at the same meeting. The CEO was fine with that, but he made it clear that he wants a decision by early next week, and the work needs to begin soon after that."

Bill also shared that other near-term acquisitions may be in the works, emphasizing that delaying a decision was just not an option.

"The last thing I need to worry about is even more acquisitions," he sighed, smiling grimly.

Paul and Susan sat in stunned silence. Neither had anticipated this turn of events. Just like that, the account team now faced a Herculean effort, with fewer than three days to prepare Agile's proposal presentation for the steering committee. If nothing else, this confirmed Paul's suspicion that MFS represented a lot more potential than the Worldwide integration alone, and if Agile lost this deal, there would be little to no chance of winning future work. What's more, the outcome of the deal could directly and immediately impact his career.

Paul gathered his wits and refocused on the original meeting objectives. But first he would deal with the proposal logistics.

"We will be ready to present this Friday," he said to Bill,

"but I need some details. For starters, how much time will we have?"

Bill figured an hour was enough time, but Paul countered that ninety minutes would be better, as it would allow for questions. He was fine either way, as long as Agile and JCN had the same amount of time. Bill agreed and asked Susan to schedule the presentations for Friday and alert the other members of the steering committee as well as JCN. The MFS steering committee consisted of Susan, Bill, Jack Grossman (VP of technology), and **Stephanie Holder** (senior procurement manager). These were the key players who would ultimately make the decision. Bill informed Paul and Susan that a few direct-report staff would also most likely be there.

"Jack Grossman is a big fan of JCN," Bill said pointedly to Paul, "so you have your work cut out convincing Jack that Agile is the best solution. For her part, Stephanie is basically neutral, but she will be the person Agile deals with if this gets to a contract and negotiation."

"I haven't met Jack," Paul responded. "Aside from a JCN win, can you tell me what might be important to him?"

"Jack is currently filling in for the MFS CIO, who just left the position," Bill obliged. "But recent turnover in the IT department has left him understaffed, and he's very concerned about the man-hours required to complete the integration, not to mention the technical capabilities of his inexperienced staff. Anything Agile can do to minimize the burden and disruption to Jack's team will be a positive."

"Jack's also very concerned about the aggressive schedule demanded by the board of directors," Susan volunteered.

This information about Jack was invaluable, and it played nicely into the strategy Paul had devised with his team. Now, with the logistics of the proposal presentation out of the way, Paul needed to turn his attention to validating Bill's priorities and the remaining buying steps.

"Bill, I also want to be sure I understand *your* priorities. Based on our work to date, here is what we understand. First, the MFS sales organization needs *complete access* to the Worldwide databases and applications. Second, the integration *must be completed* by the board's deadline. Third, it must be completed *under budget*. Is this list right, or what did I miss? Also, how should we rank these as priorities?"

"That's my list as far as IT is concerned," Bill confirmed, "and as to priorities, timeline is most important, followed by access, and then budget."

"Great. Thank you," Paul responded. "Now, what about

the expectations and implications for these requirements? More than anything, this is the information my team will need to put together a competitive presentation. For instance, would it be beneficial if Agile completed the Worldwide integration well ahead of the board's schedule?"

Bill broke into a broad grin and said it would make him a hero at MFS. Certainly, the CEO would get off his back, and the CFO would be thrilled! In his earlier meeting with the CEO, Bill had shared that MFS expected to generate at least $10 million to $15 million per month in incremental operating profits as soon as the Worldwide data and applications were available.

"But I still haven't heard any specifics on *how far ahead* of the board's deadline," Bill deadpanned.

"We've got a little more work to do on that, but this Friday you'll get specific timelines that you can bank on," Paul countered, pressing on. "And to help us make that presentation as complete as possible, we were wondering, are any of Worldwide's applications or data more important than others?"

"That's a great question, and as far as I know, nobody has looked at it that way," Bill confessed; then, jotting a note, "I'll put that one to my team and get back to you."

"I'll wave my consulting fee on that one," Paul said wryly, and they all chuckled, but it was not lost on him that he was asking questions that demonstrated both forethought and a problem-solving mindset. "OK, last question," he continued. "How important is it to the budget that we reduce or delay any hardware purchases?"

Bill looked down for a long moment, tapping his finger on the arm of his chair.

"All right, I'm going to spill a few beans here, pun intended," he finally said. "My budget for the integration is over $120 million. But before anyone gets too excited, only a fraction of that applies to the IT integration. In any case, as of now the budget is not an issue, with or without the hardware purchases."

Good to know, Paul thought to himself, filing the information under "confidential." He was sure now that Agile's focus on value (time), rather than cost savings, was the right approach and that JCN's apparent cost-only strategy might not necessarily be to their advantage. Also, Agile would be best served by downplaying any cost benefit relative to the implementation schedule.

With Bill's priorities vetted, Paul turned his attention to the remaining buying steps for MFS. He confirmed that the first step was the proposal itself, and today's meeting was a huge help in refining Friday's presentation. He asked if the formal written proposal, which would normally be submitted at the time of the presentation, could be delivered the following week. Bill readily agreed, given the abnormally tight deadline Paul and his team now faced, adding that MFS needed the proposal as soon after Friday as possible.

"So let's assume that Agile wins the day on Friday," Paul said, "and the written proposal goes through. I'm very fond of this assumption, by the way." He laughed as Bill and Susan smiled. "What is the next step?"

"Ah, that's the one that worries me most," Bill responded, "getting contractual Ts and Cs sorted out with MFS legal, not to mention commercial terms, like price and payment terms, with procurement."

Paul struggled to respond to Bill's concern, given that it presented a legitimate potential obstacle to completing the integration on time. But Susan quickly came to the rescue.

"We're in a push to convert key existing Worldwide contracts to direct contracts with MFS," she stated. "Both legal departments are working on that right now."

She committed to having the Agile contract bumped to

the front of the line and ensured that it was a top priority. Paul volunteered to put his legal representative, Caroline Borders, in touch with MFS to help speed the process.

"Well, that's much better!" Bill laughed. "I need to have more meetings with you two! But seriously, I want to be sure that JCN and Agile are competing on a level playing field, and I'd hate for contract technicalities to be a deal breaker for Agile."

"One technicality we can't avoid," he continued, "is nego-tiating the commercial terms with MFS procurement. I may be responsible for the more strategic side of the negotiation, but procurement is charged with getting the best price for MFS. So, Paul, you can expect to be 'taken to the woodshed,' especially by Stephanie Holder, the senior procurement manager on the steering committee. If everyone survives that process, a purchase order will be issued within a couple of days and the work will begin!"

Paul confirmed that the remaining buying steps were 1) Friday's proposal presentation to the steering committee, followed by a formal written proposal, 2) establishment of contract terms and conditions between MFS and Agile legal, 3) negotiation of commercial terms with MFS procurement, and 4) issuance of a purchase order. He thanked Bill for his time and Susan for all her help. They agreed that the presentation on Friday was key to

Agile's success, and they looked forward to seeing each other then.

Paul left the meeting certain that Susan was a strong supporter and sponsor of Agile, and he was beginning to believe that Bill may also be leaning Agile's way. He and the team had done their homework, and with Susan's help, his value proposition crisply answered why Bill and MFS should care. It also clearly laid out the incremental value Agile was proposing and exactly what they would deliver. And of course, the answer to the question, *why now?* could not have been more obvious: time was of the essence, and only Agile could bring a successful solution to bear within the board's time frame. Everything would hinge on how good Paul and his team made Bill look to the board and CEO.

On his way back to the office, Paul got a surprise call from Susan. "Listen, I've got another call in a few minutes, but I need to share one breaking thing with you—and it's important. MFS announced just this afternoon that we're also acquiring American Investment Corporation (AIC). AIC is a niche player, similar to Worldwide, but the reason this matters is that AIC's IT department is *completely outsourced to JCN.*"

Paul was momentarily stunned, but he quickly refocused on his driving. *I just can't catch a break,* he thought.

Susan explained that Paul and his team would obviously need to consider AIC's integration in their approach and that as soon as her team had gathered technical specs of the integration, she would send them to his sales engineer, Jane Jones, so that she and her team could properly scope the work.

"Paul, I hate to say it, but the AIC acquisition will be a big gust of wind in JCN's sails," she concluded on a somber note.

"Well, I guess it's time to gas up the powerboat," Paul chuckled half-heartedly. Now the account team had even more to contend with and precious little time to prepare for an outstanding proposal presentation and, with any luck, for the negotiation with procurement.

"Talk about a fast-moving target!" Paul said to himself after the call. This would easily be the most important proposal presentation of his career.

Summary

There's no question that selling in the B2B world is complicated. And it is only getting more challenging—especially if you keep selling the way you always have. Customers today have access to much more information about you, your business, and your offerings. They also have more access to *your* customers. In a way, this is good news; as salespeople, we no longer need to be "two-legged sales brochures," and we can focus on more high-value activities. The most important step in any customer's decision process (and something they will never be able to Google) is determining *which supplier knows them the best*. Who understands the problems they are trying to solve, the opportunities they are trying to seize? And who understands the outcomes they want to achieve?

Selling is nothing more than ensuring that we are not wasting the customer's valuable time, but rather are focusing on creating the potential for value for them. Thus, value is the currency of sales, as well as negotiations and eventually account management after the sale. Effectively discovering and then presenting value in an irresistible value proposition is critical to the success of any sales campaign. The best value propositions are linked to one or more high priorities of the key decision makers (because that is what they are focused on), shine a spotlight on the incremental value of your offering, and are couched in the customer's language (so they can clearly see the potential outcomes). Remember, how the customer will measure success when achieving any outcome is how they will also ultimately measure value. Using their language makes it that much easier for the customer to choose you. The case story may be fictional, but it depicts a realistic scenario where a tightly crafted value proposition can quickly shift the conversation from proving value to planning the solution.

The next book in this series, *The Compelling Proposal*, showcases the proposal as a strategic tool to reinforce trust and credibility, making it easy for the customer to buy from you, trust their choice, and manage the uncertainty inherent in the real world. Keep reading to find out how Paul and his team develop their proposal presentation for the steering committee at MFS. Will they be able to navigate political landmines and deal with potentially hostile members of the steering committee? Does JCN have more surprises in store for the Agile team?

My goal in writing this book is to help you to see that how you position your offering (your value proposition) is just as important as the solution itself, if not more so. This is consistent with my observations, time and again, that how you sell and negotiate deals is more important than what you sell—a crucial point that creates real job security for talented salespeople! Remember, your goal is to build trust and credibility through your selling approach, making it easy for the customer to choose you and your company.

This book presents the essential steps to developing an irresistible value proposition. Since we now know that value is both specific to the customer's situation and always incremental to their alternative, it is critical that you become adept at analyzing the customer's most likely alternative to you—for that is what you are really competing against. To that end, I have created a generic *Alternative Impacts* table (see the appendix) that you can use when analyzing both your alternative and the customer's alternative. While the items in this version are applicable to most businesses, it is by no means complete, but it should give you a good place to start. Every business (and industry) has its own language and items that are particular to that business, so you'll have to "fill in the blanks" and customize it for your needs.

You can also download an electronic copy of the same

Alternative Impacts table from my website, valuelifecycle. com. While there, you may also want to check out the quirky video we produced explaining business value. Most salespeople find it both fun and informative.

As a final bonus for you, I have developed a companion workshop to this book. Also called *The Irresistible Value Proposition*, the workshop is available online at mustwindeals.valuelifecycle.com. If you're interested in working on a live opportunity applying the concepts in these pages— something I highly recommend—please check it out. The two tiers include a standalone workshop and a second version that includes one-on-one coaching from me on your live value proposition. I am pleased to offer you a significant discount on both tiers as a *thank-you* for buying this book. Just enter the promotion code "Book219" to get your discount—and thanks for being a customer!

How's that for value?

Good selling!

About the Author

STEVE THOMPSON is managing partner at Value Lifecycle™, which helps companies position, negotiate, and close critical business deals. In the past twenty years, he has worked on more than $15 billion in B2B deals in over 120 different industries. He previously worked in senior operations, sales, and executive management at Westinghouse, Black & Decker, and DuPont. Steve also served as a nuclear submarine officer in the US Navy.

Appendix

EXAMPLES OF ALTERNATIVE IMPACTS
Analyzing What Each Side Must Accept If There Is No Deal

	TANGIBLE IMPACTS		INTANGIBLE IMPACTS
Seller Alternative	• Revenue (-) • Commission (-) • Quota / Goals (-) • Opportunity Costs (-) • Market Share (-) • Reference Account (-)	• President's Club (-) • Up-sell Potential Revenue (-) • Maintain Pricing Integrity (+) • Unprofitable Deal (+)	• Relationship with Customer (-) • Personal Political Hit (-) • Corporate Market Image (-) • Difficult to re-enter Account (-) • "Ripple" Effect on Other Customers (-) • Personal / Team Confidence (-) • Internal Relationships / Credibility (-)
Buyer Alternative	• Switching Costs (+/-) • Discount (+/-) • Meet Budget (+/-) • Functionality (+/-) • Integration (+/-) • Scalability (+/-) • Support Costs (+/-)	• Time to Implement (+/-) • Operational Impacts (+/-) • Regulatory Compliance (+/-) • Breadth of Solutions (+/-) • SLAs (+/-) • Key Influencer(s) MBO, Bonus, Promotion (+/-)	• Risk of change (+/-) • User Acceptance (+/-) • Politics (+/-) • Perception of Quality (+/-) • Flexibility (+/-) • Personal / Business Relationships (+/-) • Corporate Image (+/-) • Branding Message (+/-)